Sketches and Lyrics from
INTIMACY AT EIGHT-THIRTY

by David Climie, Peter Myers,
Alec Grahame

Music by
John Pritchett, Ronald Cass
and Norman Dannatt

SAMUEL FRENCH

Copyright © 1956 by Samuel French Ltd
All Rights Reserved

INTIMACY AT EIGHT-THIRTY is fully protected under the copyright laws of the British Commonwealth, including Canada, the United States of America, and all other countries of the Copyright Union. All rights, including professional and amateur stage productions, recitation, lecturing, public reading, motion picture, radio broadcasting, television, online/digital production, and the rights of translation into foreign languages are strictly reserved.

ISBN 978-0-573-07012-9

concordtheatricals.co.uk
concordtheatricals.com

FOR AMATEUR PRODUCTION ENQUIRIES

UNITED KINGDOM AND WORLD
EXCLUDING NORTH AMERICA
licensing@concordtheatricals.co.uk
020-7054-7298

Each title is subject to availability from Concord Theatricals, depending upon country of performance.

CAUTION: Professional and amateur producers are hereby warned that *INTIMACY AT EIGHT-THIRTY* is subject to a licensing fee. The purchase, renting, lending or use of this book does not constitute a licence to perform this title(s), which licence must be obtained from the appropriate agent prior to any performance. Performance of this title(s) without a licence is a violation of copyright law and may subject the producer and/or presenter of such performances to penalties. Both amateurs and professionals considering a production are strongly advised to apply to the appropriate agent before starting rehearsals, advertising, or booking a theatre. A licensing fee must be paid whether the title is presented for charity or gain and whether or not admission is charged.

This work is published by Samuel French, an imprint of Concord Theatricals Ltd.

The Professional Rights in this play are controlled by Concord Theatricals, Aldwych House, 71-91 Aldwych, London, WC2B 4HN, UK .

No one shall make any changes in this title for the purpose of production. No part of this book may be reproduced, stored in a retrieval system, scanned, uploaded, or transmitted in any form, by any means, now known or yet to be invented, including mechanical, electronic, digital, photocopying, recording, videotaping, or otherwise, without the prior written permission of the publisher. No one shall share this title, or part of this title, to any social media or file hosting websites.

The moral right of David Climie, Peter Myers, Alec Grahame to be identified as author of this work has been asserted in accordance with Section 77 of the Copyright, Designs and Patents Act 1988.

USE OF COPYRIGHTED MUSIC

A licence issued by Concord Theatricals to perform this play does not include permission to use the incidental music specified in this publication. In the United Kingdom: Where the place of performance is already licensed by the PERFORMING RIGHT SOCIETY (PRS) a return of the music used must be made to them. If the place of performance is not so licensed then application should be made to PRS for Music (www.prsformusic.com). A separate and additional licence from PHONOGRAPHIC PERFORMANCE LTD (www.ppluk.com) may be needed whenever commercial recordings are used. Outside the United Kingdom: Please contact the appropriate music licensing authority in your territory for the rights to any incidental music.

USE OF COPYRIGHTED THIRD-PARTY MATERIALS

Licensees are solely responsible for obtaining formal written permission from copyright owners to use copyrighted third-party materials (e.g., artworks, logos) in the performance of this play and are strongly cautioned to do so. If no such permission is obtained by the licensee, then the licensee must use only original materials that the licensee owns and controls. Licensees are solely responsible and liable for clearances of all third-party copyrighted materials, and shall indemnify the copyright owners of the play(s) and their licensing agent, Concord Theatricals Ltd., against any costs, expenses, losses and liabilities arising from the use of such copyrighted third-party materials by licensees.

IMPORTANT BILLING AND CREDIT REQUIREMENTS

If you have obtained performance rights to this title, please refer to your licensing agreement for important billing and credit requirements.

CONTENTS

Knit Yourself a Lost Weekend	page 1
Coach and Five	4
Fit to be Tied	6
Siren Song	8
Sustained Objection	10
Earliest Editions	12
Business in Great Waters	14
Soft Shoe Shuffle	16
We Come Up from Mummerset	18
Peter Patter	24

KNIT YOURSELF A LOST WEEKEND

by

DAVID CLIMIE

from an idea by

GEORGE WADMORE

Characters

MRS TROUT	*Joan Sims*
ROSIE	*Pip Hinton*
FRED	*Hugh Paddick*
BERT	*Ron Moody*
COMPÈRE	

COMPÈRE. Ladies and gentlemen—a theory has been advanced recently that the influence of alcohol is mainly psychological—that good company—a friendly atmosphere and the determination to have a good time—all these things are far more intoxicating than drink. So, since alcohol is apparently unnecessary it seems quite accidental that the centre of our social life should be the public house. Supposing it weren't? Would the pub-going public gather somewhere else? Would the habits, behaviour and conversation of the pub spring up in some environment that seems inappropriate to us now? We think so. As follows . . .

(*The scene is a wool shop represented by a counter with two sweaters on stands. Beside the counter is a chair. The counter and anywhere else practicable is festooned with posters reading:* "WOOL IS GOOD FOR YOU", "WOOL FOR STRENGTH", "THERE IS NO SUBSTITUTE FOR WOOL", "WOOL IS BEST", "HAVE A FAIRISLE JUMPER WHEN YOU'RE TIRED". MRS TROUT, *a gloomy old pub habituée, is seated on the chair by the counter, knitting and mumbling to herself. Behind the counter, leaning indolently on it and primping her hair is* ROSIE, *a pert barmaid type. Both* ROSIE *and* MRS TROUT *wear plain frocks*)

MRS TROUT. Very quiet tonight, ennit, Rosie?
ROSIE. Bit early for 'em yet, Mrs Trout. They'll be in—don't you worry.

(FRED MORRIS *enters. He wears slacks, a shirt with no collar and slippers only*)

ROSIE. Oh, yais—'ere's the old faithful Mr Morris.
MRS TROUT. Might 'ave known it. First in—last out—that's Fred Morris. Dunno what 'e does with 'isself on early closin' day.
FRED. Nah then, Ma—don't be saucy. 'Ullo, Rosie, ducks. (*He chucks her under the chin*)
ROSIE. 'Evenin' Mr Morris. Usual?
FRED. Yerse. Just a small sweater, please.

(ROSIE *hands him one from under the counter*)

(*taking it*) Well, first today! (*He holds it up for a moment in toast*) Cheers!
ROSIE. Up your jumper!
FRED (*slipping it on in one movement*) Ah—that's better. I'll 'ave the other 'arf of that.

(ROSIE *hands him another sweater*)

(*As he puts it on*) 'Ave something yourself, Rosie, won't you?
ROSIE. Not now, Mr Morris. But I'll 'ave a small pullover if I may. (*She takes one from under the counter and climbs into it*)
FRED. 'Ow about you, Mrs Trout?
ROSIE (*holding up one*) Yes, why don't you try a Fairisle, Mrs Trout?
MRS TROUT. No, dear—not a cocktail. I like them, but they don't like me. I get a terrible 'angover soon as I put one on.
ROSIE. Well, o' course—you gotter 'ave the figure for 'em.
FRED. Which you got, eh, Rosie? Make mine a large cardigan will you, dear?
ROSIE (*serving him*) Oops—sorry—I dropped a stitch on you.

(*While* FRED *puts his cardigan on* BERT HARRIS *enters looking a bit wan. He also is wearing a shirt, trousers and slippers*)

BERT. 'Evenin', all.
ROSIE. 'Evenin', Mr 'Arris.
FRED. 'Ullo, Bert—you don't look too good.
ROSIE. Shouldn't think so after the way 'e went on in 'ere last night.
MRS TROUT. Disgustin' it was. If a man can't 'old 'is wool, I say . . .
BERT. Orright, Mrs Trout, orright. I admit it. I was as woolly as a newt.
ROSIE. Mr Harris—language!
BERT. Sorry, Rose.
FRED. Well, 'ow about a hair of the sheep that bit you, ole man?
BERT. No, no, this is mine, Fred. Better make mine a small Balaclava, Rosie.
FRED. Same for me, Rose.

INTIMACY AT EIGHT-THIRTY

(ROSIE *hands over two Balaclava helmets*)

ROSIE (*to* FRED) You're mixin' 'em a bit, Mr Morris, ain't you?

FRED (*a little slurred and belligerent, as he puts on his helmet*) Thass all right, gel. I can look after meself. You never seen me the worse for wool.

BERT (*putting on his helmet*) 'Ow about you, Mrs T? I see your needles are nearly empty.

MRS TROUT. That's very kind of you, Mr 'Arris. I wouldn't say no to a little something to keep the chill out. I'll 'ave a long vest.

(ROSIE *hands over a vest which* MRS TROUT *gets into it over her dress*)

FRED (*singing*) Wool, wool, glorious wool— Buy it till wardrobes are full.

ROSIE. No singin' in the shop, *if* you don't mind, Mr Morris.

FRED. I don't care—I'll 'ave a pair of socks. Big ones!

ROSIE (*handing over some football stockings which* FRED *proceeds to don uncertainly*) I reckon you've 'ad enough, Mr Morris.

FRED (*unheedingly singing*) Ha, ha, ha, he, he, he—li'l brown socks don' I love thee?

ROSIE. No singin' in the shop, *if* you please!

MRS TROUT. I'll 'ave me nightcap and be off, I think.

ROSIE. Orright, Mrs Trout.

(*She hands over a woollen nightcap which* MRS TROUT *dons. Then she furtively hands her a roll of magazines which* MRS TROUT *furtively puts in her bag and goes out, avoiding* FRED *ostentatiously*)

ROSIE }
BERT } 'Night, Mrs Trout.

FRED. Ni', Mrs Trou'.

(MRS TROUT *exits. A bell rings*)

ROSIE. Time, gents, please! Time! Kindly finish your garments. Button up, please. Cast off, please. (*To* BERT) You'd better get 'im 'ome, Mr 'Arris.

FRED. I'll be all right. I'll just nip round to the pub for a couple of double whiskies.

ROSIE. Double whiskies? Whatever for?

FRED. What for? Blimey, there wouldn't 'arf be a row if I went 'ome to the wife smelling of wool!

BLACK-OUT

COACH AND FIVE

Words by *Music by*
PETER MYERS & ALEC GRAHAME   JOHN PRITCHETT

Characters

A North Country Family
MUM   SON
DAD   DAUGHTER
AUNTIE

These parts were played by

Joan Sims   *Hugh Paddick*
Ronnie Stevens   *Pip Hinton*

ALL. This year, just for a change,
We gave Morecambe a miss;
All our friends have stopped going there,
The thing to do is this . . .

All round Europe in a chara,
On a Fourteen Day Coach Tour;
DAD. Such cosmopolitan people you meet,
A fellow from Sheffield was sharing my seat.
SON. Our first night was merry,
Boiled beef on the ferry,
And the waiter called Father "*Monsieur*";
MUM. We simply loved Brussels and Bayreuth was swell,
SON. A tenor sang *Parsifal* ever so well,
DAD. As an encore we asked him for *Eskimo Nell*,
ALL. On our jolly Holiday Tour.

AUNT. In Brussels I bought some sprouts. In Cologne I bought some *eau*. In Switzerland I bought a watch. And in Austria I bought a zither.

ALL. All round Europe in a chara,
MUM. Venice smells so very pure;
SON. The sea on the Lido is ever so blue,
But they haven't got rock lettered Venice all through.

INTIMACY AT EIGHT-THIRTY

MUM. And after our auntie,
Had tried some chianti,
On the Campanile roof she took poor;
DAUGHTER. We saw an Art Gallery out in Cremona,
MUM. One picture called Lisa; another called Mona,
DAD and SON.
And we used the two gentlemens of Verona,
ALL. On our jolly Holiday Tour.

AUNT. In Venice I bought a plastic ashtray in the shape of a gondola. In Sorrento I bought a musical box playing—guess what?

ALL. All round Europe in a chara,
MUM. Paris, city of l'amour;
DAUGHTER. Those Existentialists—ee, I was kissed,
Then they revealed to me why I exist.
MUM. On the Grand Boulevard,
I was offered a card,
When I looked at it—it was impure!
DAD. In London we saw a show when we were there,
Six girls standing still with their top halfs all bare,
SON. They've got it in France now, that Folies Bergère,
ALL. On our jolly Holiday Tour.

AUNT. In Paris I bought a funny hat saying *"Chassez-moi, Charlie, je suis le dernier autobus chez"*.

DAD. Then we had some bad luck,
For them ruddy French struck,
And the bus driver did us, what's more;
MUM. He was bribed by rich tourists to ferry them out,
SON. We would have been stuck there without any doubt,
AUNT. Except that I sold a funny hat, a musical box, a
plastic ashtray, a zither, a watch, some *eau*
and one brussel sprout. . . .
ALL. On Our Jolly Holiday Tour.

BLACK-OUT

FIT TO BE TIED

Words by　　　　　　　*Music by*
DAVID CLIMIE　　　　JOHN PRITCHETT

Characters

A SPIV　　　*Peter Felgate*
A GIRL　　　*Eleanor Fazan*

(*A drape-shaped* SPIV *is discovered before the Tabs*)

I guess I'm not what you'd call the romantic type;
Not the kind to do me nut I can't deny;
But love's sweet and tender passion in its customary fashion
Has been and gone and done me in the eye.
Though I know it's kind of stupid to be thinking about Cupid
When you push a barrer Cambridge Circus way—
It was there that I first met her—by the Tatler News Theatre
And I loved her as I love her still today—
That lovely little lady, who, by exercise of art
Flew just like an arrer to a barrer-boy's heart . . .

(*The Tabs open on a luscious* GIRL *who is dressed in a Bikini, an Eton collar and bow tie, with high-heeled slippers. She is perched on a bar stool and is holding a champagne glass*)

I'm in love with the girl on the hand-painted tie!
And I fell just as quick as you please;
Though I did but see her while passing by
The shop window of Cecil Gee's.
Though she wore no silk hose and no fancy clothes—
Leastways none you could actually see—
That little old teeny-weeny Bikini
Spelt love in big letters to me.
You can tell she's a scholar by her Eton collar
And as far above me as the sky—
Still I could aspire to buy her and tie her—
The girl on the hand painted tie.

(*The* GIRL *dances*)

I'm in love with the girl on the hand-painted tie
From her head to her hand-painted toes;
There's something about her that caught my eye—

It must be something that shows.
The photographs round her the day that I found her
Seemed to say "You Presumptious Fool"
Alan Ladds in Fedoras all echoed this chorus—
Robert Mitchum in spear points looked cool.
Still, we met face to face—a transaction took place,
And I think we both felt rather shy
When I paid twelve and nine and so made her mine—
The girl on the hand-painted tie.

I'm in love with the girl on the hand-painted tie;
Though the years have gone by they won't spoil
The mem'ry of her who was always my
Ideal of beauty in oil.
Though our time was so short, I still treasure the thought
Of our courtship and love—for in spite
Of the fact she was mute, I could still press my suit
With her 'neath the mattress at night.
And when I was dressed she would lay on my chest—
But a love such as ours had to die;
Till she chipped off I wore her—I'll always adore her
The girl on the hand-painted tie!

SIREN SONG

Words by　　　　　　　　　　　　　　　　*Music by*
DAVID CLIMIE　　　　　　　　　　　　JOHN PRITCHETT

Character

A WOMAN　　　*Joan Sims*

The announcement should be breathed into a live microphone if possible

When I was young, the height of my ambition
Was to be a thorough-going *femme fatale*;
I wanted to lure men into positions
Where they'd gladly offer me the Taj Mahal.
Alas, among life's flurry and its hubbub,
My great ambition seemed to drift away;
Now I'm working on a station in a subbub,
Announcing train arrivals every day.
But still I think of what I'd be if I could have the choice
And my frustrated sex appeal just creeps into my voice . . .

When I say "Woking Woking"—
It's thoroughly provoking
To the men who travel up from platform two;
I just say "This is Woking"
But the thoughts that I'm invoking
Keep them panting till they get to Waterloo.
It's more the way I say it than the actual things I say;
They may be great big business men but in my hands they're clay;
For City gents all faint when I say "There's a slight delay"
They're the victims of the Golden Voice.

When I say "Woking Woking"
Stokers stop their stoking
And lumps of coal drop from each nerveless hand;
I just say "Have your seasons ready" and it makes them quite
　　　　　　　　　　　　　　　　　　　　　　unsteady;
Could it be that they misunderstand?
I remember once a Bishop and a graduate Collegian
Just caught my voice as they were going through the Southern
　　　　　　　　　　　　　　　　　　　　　　Region;
They were later found in Tunis where they'd joined the Foreign
　　　　　　　　　　　　　　　　　　　　　　Legion—
They were victims of the Golden Voice.

When I say "Platform Four" it means a great deal more
And embarrasses the early morning rush;
For I make the eight fifteen sound thoroughly obscene
And when I say "Alight for Bagshot", well, even porters blush.

When I say "Woking Woking" Stockbrokers stop their broking
And commercial travellers stop their little games;
I just say "This is Woking" and in carriages marked "Smoking"
They not only smoke, they all burst into flames.
But though of course I sympathize with masculine frustration
I can't encourage them for there's a Railway Regulation
Which frowns on all—activity while standing in the Station,
And so of course they have no choice—
They're victims of the Golden Voice—
"All change for Esher, Haslemere, Virginia Water and
    all connections to Maidenhead."
They're the victims of the Golden Voice.

SUSTAINED OBJECTION

Words by *Music by*
DAVID CLIMIE RONALD CASS

Characters

A JUDGE   Hngh Paddick
A LADY Q.C.

A querulous old JUDGE *is discovered seated behind a Judge's high bench. He is in full robes and wig and wears his spectacles on the end of his nose. Strewn around him are large, legal-looking volumes, scrolls of parchment with seals and note pads. He is peering into the volumes and scrolls and is scribbling on a pad.*

I suppose you think I'm making learned notes here?
Well, I'm not—I'm writing out a vulgar rhyme;
In this deed all tucked away
Are the works of Rabelais—
That's why I glance at it from time to time.
And sometimes you will catch me taking surreptitious looks—
I'm reading all the dirty bits in all the Statute Books.
I know it's reprehensible, but my defence is short—
I find it's more amusing than what goes on in the Court . . .

    For I never get the *interesting* cases—
    And by "interesting" you know what I mean.
    Though other Judges deal in vice,
    And crimes that aren't considered—"nice"
    I get the kind that's heard but *not* obscene.
    Other judges get vivacious
    Over all the sweet salacious
    Little details of the cases of the day;
    But pity us poor Benchers
    Who get nothing more licentious
    Than the wrong sort of disputed Right of Way.
    Instead of a nice little sordid seduction
    I get Tribunals on Rental Reduction.
    It makes me simply furious
    That vices known as—"curious"
    Don't seem to be requiring my decree;
    I would love a case so juicy

It embarrasses the Q.C.
But they never give a juicy case to me.

Why I never get the interesting cases
Is something I shall never understand;
I know two things about divorce
And both of them are rather coarse
But both I had to learn at second hand.
While Mr Justice Lavory
Gets cases of white slavery
Lord Croom gets choir masters who default,
And Mr Justice Rattery
Gets lovely bits of battery
And tasty little pinches of assault.
But *my* Court's always empty—you can't tempt the visitors
When the only soliciting's done by solicitors.
Although I'd love to hammer a
Decision out in camera
With photographs passed up for me to see—
I am sure I could be trusted
To be properly disgusted
But they never give a juicy case to me!

Oh, I never get the interesting cases;
I never get the cases that enthrall;
The people *I* get in my dock
Just never seem to run amuck
And hardly ever change their sex at all.
Why should the others get all of the prizes?
I'm sick to death of these Bloody Assizes!
This unfair discrimination
Has produced such desperation
That although it's not judicious I agree,
Ev'ry dog must have his one day—
I'll be in the papers Sunday—
For there's going to be a juicy case—you'll see.

(*A* LADY Q.C. *enters, in gown and wig, and crosses*)

    (*Speaking*) Miss Fortescue—will you go to my chambers?
    There's something I wish to discuss with you.

(*She smiles, nods, crosses and exits*)

    (*Singing*) Yes—there's going to be a juicy case—it's *me*!

BLACK-OUT

EARLIEST EDITIONS

Words by
PETER MYERS, ALEC GRAHAME
and DAVID CLIMIE

Music by
RONALD CASS

Characters

THREE BABIES   *Joan Heal, Hugh Paddick & Joan Sims*

Three BABIES *are discovered sitting in high chairs. On the table pieces in front they have piles of newspapers and magazines.*

ALL. Hush-a-bye, baby
Cease all your capers
Sit down and study the junior papers.
The *Junior Mirror* has been a success
So here are some others come hot from the press.

(To a skipping beat)

1ST BABY. The *Junior Times*,
2ND BABY. The *Junior Worker*,
3RD BABY. The *Junior Statesman & Nation!*
2ND BABY. Bob-a-job scandal, Tory outrages!
Scouts can't exist on these starvation wages.
1ST BABY. Gob stopper prices are up again
Big pocket money inflation.
3RD BABY. Film censors should make a new code for the screen
Cert. "Y" for "*Beau Brummell*" and others we've seen
"Not fit to be shown to those over sixteen"
ALL. Read the *Junior Times*, the *Junior Worker*, the *Junior Statesman & Nation!*

3RD BABY. Excerpt from the correspondence column of the *Junior Times*. "Sir, it may be unsporting to suggest this; but could the defeat of the British team in Moscow be due to the fact that the Russians bake their conkers?—Yours, etc., Horatio Nelson, R.N. retired."

ALL. Then there's . . .
3RD BABY. The *Junior Tatler*,
2ND BABY. The *Junior Vogue*,
1ST BABY. The *Junior Woman & Home*.

INTIMACY AT EIGHT-THIRTY

2ND BABY. Noted in Bond Street, platinum crib,
Monogrammed pusher and tiny mink bib.
1ST BABY. Musical instruments, make it yourself,
Long-playing paper and comb.
No pages and pages of debs to appal
2ND BABY. Our pages and pages of pages enthrall
1ST BABY. We've Crawfie's life story—"Two Youngsters tell all"
ALL. Read the *Junior Tatler*, the *Junior Vogue*, the *Junior Woman & Home!*

1ST BABY. A letter to Nanny Drew—"I am a young girl aged four and a half, but well-developed for my age. Every day my teacher walks me home from school. He is twenty-six. Do you think this disparity in ages will mar our future happiness? Yours truly, Troubled Blue Eyes."

ALL. But best of all there's . . .
1ST BABY. The *Junior People*,
2ND BABY. The *Junior Pic*,
3RD BABY. And the *Junior News of the World*.
2ND BABY. Vice in a playground. Horrible things.
Girl picked up on roundabouts—lost it on swings.
1ST BABY. Piggy bank robbed; marks of violence on slot
Vile accusations are hurled.
2ND BABY. Mandy Miller in 3 D—Swindon protested.
1ST BABY. Rubber duck drowned in bath; foul play suspected.
3RD BABY. Tramp murdered in woods; three-year-old girl arrested.
ALL. Read the *Junior People*, the *Junior Pic* and the *Junior News of the World!*

2ND BABY. Letter to the Editor, *Junior News of the World*. "Dear Sir, Since your disgusting serial, *The Sex Life of Noddy in Toyland*, I have been forced to ban your paper from my house. Suppose it was left lying around and my innocent parents picked it up? Yours, Mother of Twelve Dollies, Huddersfield."

ALL. What next will we kiddies be offered to read?
Here's the answer before you can ask it.
1ST BABY. If this trend continues—and that's how it looks
2ND BABY. They'll soon give us junior versions of books
3RD BABY. We're all of us longing to fasten our hooks
1ST BABY. On *The Daughter of Amber*
2ND BABY. *The Son of Miss Blandish*
3RD BABY. And *Lady Chatterly's Basket!*

BLACK-OUT

BUSINESS IN GREAT WATERS

Words by
DAVID CLIMIE

Music by
JOHN PRITCHETT

Characters

THREE LITERARY SAILORS   *Ronnie Stevens, Digby Wolfe & Ron Moody*

To be sung by a trio of bearded and possibly duffle-coated Naval officers. Their attitude is one of stiff-upper-lipped correctness, alternating with a kind of maniac jocularity. Lines to be split accordingly.

Three old sea-dogs!
Three old he-dogs!
Three old jolly old sons of she-dogs!
Three old Barnacle Bills come back from sea!
Three old war-dogs!
Three, not four, dogs!
Three old jolly old ship not shore dogs!
Three in the upper income groups are we!
For though we never ruled the waves and we're no Captain Cooks
We're no fools—we waived the rules,
And we all wrote Naval Books!

We're three rollicking literary sailors!
Three lovable literary tars!
Though the war was quite exciting we just got on with our writing
And hitched our battlewagons to our literary stars!
In the frisky Bay of Biscay when things got a little risky
I lashed myself to my shift key.
We went through quite a fair amount of action we confess;
But when it was and where it was we none of us could guess,
For we couldn't hear the firing for the typing in the mess
While sailing on the Cruel, Cruel Sea!

> I must go down to the seas again
> To the lonely days and the nights;
> And all I ask is a small advance,
> And the second serial rights!

Oh, we're three rollicking literary sailors!
Writing of the things that sailors do.

While patrolling our Dependencies some psychopathic tendencies
Were shown by certain independent members of my crew.
I said "Go on and mutiny—I don't care what you do to me—
It's what I need for Chapter Three".
I can't forget the fateful day a Channel port we took;
I hoisted up a signal as we sailed around the Hook—
"England expects this day that every man will write a book—"
A book about the Cruel, Cruel Sea!

> Columbus sailed the ocean blue
> In fourteen hundred and ninety-two.
> But on the whole we had more sport
> With a publisher in every port.

Oh, we're three rollicking literary sailors!
Writing of the days when men were men;
For the kind of books we retail are the kind which speak in detail
Of the more engrossing biological aspects of the WREN.
Obscenity—profanity—we write of with urbanity,
And naval slang's our cup of repartee.
We can't forget the comradeship we simple sailors had;
And when the war was over—well, I guess we all felt sad.
1st SAILOR. Why don't we all sign on again?
2nd & 3rd SAILORS.   You must be bloody mad!
We're finished with the Cruel, Cruel Sea!
It's so commercial!
We're so grateful to the Kind, Cruel Sea!

SOFT SHOE SHUFFLE

Words by *Music by*
Peter Myers & Alec Grahame Norman Dannatt

Characters

A Man *Peter Felgate*
A Woman *Joan Sims*

We are not so very fond of modern music
I suppose you'd say that all we were out of key
But it seems that all these sambas and these be-bops
Are a bit too complicated for me.
For we've an affection for the songs they used to sing
When the minstrels gave the audience a thrill
Mr Bones and Mr Jones were comics
And Mr Interlocutor would top the bill.
I reckon nowadays you'd laugh at us as out-of-date
You'd label us as corny—well, we know
But as long as we exist
Then we never shall resist
That certain syncopation we remember with a glow—
                                        Because a . . .

Soft Shoe Shuffle
Has that old fashioned appeal
It's got a rhythm that we feel
In fact we're thinking that it's our ideal
                                        Give me some . . .

Swanee Music
A tune that's mellow and sweet
I'll be in my seventh heaven doing fine
With that hazy, lazy, lackadaisy rhythm of mine
                                        For with a . . .

Soft Shoe Shuffle
The music goes to our head, heart, hands and feet
You've got to follow the beat.

(*They dance*)

When the present hit parade is dead and gone
Then the *Lily of Laguna* will be shufflin' on
                              I love a . . .

Soft Shoe Shuffle
The music goes to our lips, hips, hands and feet
You've got to follow the . . .
    You've got to follow the . . .
        You've got to follow the beat . . .
            You've got to follow the beat.

WE COME UP FROM MUMMERSET

by

PETER MYERS, ALEC GRAHAME & DAVID CLIMIE

Characters

ANGUS	*Hugh Paddick*
HILARY	*Ronnie Stevens*
MR CROOT	*Ron Moody*
GWLADYS	*Joan Heal*
RHONA	*Joan Sims*
DYMPHNA	*Eleanor Fazan*
A YOKEL	

In front of the tabs are several tubular steel chairs. On the stage are DYMPHNA, ANGUS, GWLADYS *and* MR CROOT. DYMPHNA *is sitting cross-legged in front of the chairs, her face buried in an enormous book. She is obviously an intellectual type. She wears an immense black pageboy wig, with a fringe that comes well down over her eyes, huge spectacles, tartan or leopard skin drain-pipe slacks, a huge thick woollen sweater that comes down almost to her knees, and ballet shoes. She is surrounded by other books, spare shoes, knitting, oddly shaped parcels and a radio script.* MR CROOT *is sitting in one of the chairs. He is incredibly old, with a long, long white beard, no hair, blue spectacles, an ear trumpet and very archaic clothes. A script droops from his palsied hand.* ANGUS *is leaning against the proscenium arch, studying his script. He is also an earnest intellectual type, with a neat dark suit, woollen tie, hair parted in the middle and plastered down each side of his face, a pale complexion, a pipe drooping permanently from his mouth, a monocle and a Van Dyke beard.* GWLADYS *is a very chic and stately matron, dressed very smartly in a beautiful silk dress, enormous sables dripping from her shoulders, more jewels than a Christmas tree, a carefully arranged blue-rinse wig, with a very smart hat on it, lorgnettes, an umbrella five feet long and as thin as a pencil, and a script bound in a red morocco folder. The scene opens in silence, except for the heavy breathing of* MR CROOT *who is asleep, and the tuneless, abstracted and basso profundo humming of* DYMPHNA. *After a moment* ANGUS *consults his watch, produces a small bottle of pills and takes one. This he does at intervals throughout the sketch.* GWLADYS *looks impatiently at* DYMPHNA *but before she can speak* HILARY *hurries on to the stage. He is an extremely affected young man. He has brassy golden hair arranged in steppes up to the top of his head. He wears a brick red pair of slacks, a bright tartan shirt, a huge flowing neckerchief and a very long jade cigarette holder with a pink cigarette in it. He also carries a script. He rushes in and clutches* ANGUS's *arm contritely.*

HILARY. My dears! I'm so sorry I'm late! I had such trouble parking my little Corgi you wouldn't *believe*! That beastly commissionaire was quite abusive! Angus, you old trollop, how *are* you?

ANGUS (*moving away from him nervously*) Not very well, thank you, Hilary.

(*He takes another pill*)

HILARY (*discovering Dymphna*) And whatever is *this*? (*He bends down and parts her fringe*) Dymphna! Darling—why are you hiding?

DYMPHNA (*vaguely*) Hmmm?

HILARY. Let it pass, dear, let it pass. Good afternoon, Mr Croot!

(*There is no visible reaction from* MR CROOT)
(*He yells*) Good afternoon Mr Croot!

(*There is still no reaction*)

(*To Angus*) Dead?

GWLADYS. No more than usual.

HILARY (*turning to her*) Ah, Gladys, darling. How are we?

GWLADYS (*speaking with a very languid, drawling Kensington accent*) Very well, thank you. But I've told you before, Hilary, my name is pronounced Glay-dis—not Gladdis!

HILARY. Sorry, I'm sure.

(*They are interrupted by the arrival of* RHONA, *who is overdressed, over made-up, over-developed, and over the age of consent—a consent evidently not too jealously with-held. She has a black bubble cut, chunky jewellery and the most horrible ensemble you ever saw—something like bright yellow slacks, diamanté slippers, a Regency-striped satin blouse, elbow length gloves and a tartan tam-o-shanter. She chews gum incessantly and talks American with a Cockney accent. She carries a patent leather sling bag and a script*)

RHONA (*flicking a salute at everyone*) Greetin's gates! What's noo?

ANGUS. Ah, Rhona, my dear. Are you still with us?

RHONA. Yup. So far. But don't take no bets. They got to write me out again next week. I'm going away for the weekend.

HILARY. Brighton again?

RHONA. As a matter of fact yes!

GWLADYS. *DISGUSTING!*

RHONA. Now, look here, Gladys—

GWLADYS. *Glay*dis!
HILARY. Such affectation!
GWLADYS. It's nothing of the sort. Just because you were brought up badly it's . . .
ANGUS. Oh, I say, we don't want to bring the chap's antecedents into this, do we? I mean, sociologically speaking surely . . .
GWLADYS. Oh, shut up, you drivelling old idiot!
RHONA. Why don't *you* shut up for a change?
GWLADYS. Why, you little . . .

(*As they are screaming at one another, a bell suddenly rings. They stop immediately*)

ANGUS. Come on—we're on!

(*The tabs open, to reveal a stand microphone, with a little red bulb attached to it, in the middle of the stage. Everyone, except* MR CROOT, *rushes over and forms a group round it, clutching their scripts.* MR CROOT *sleeps peacefully on his chair*)

HILARY (*as they go to the mike*) Oh, well, back to the factory!

(*The little red light flickers on and off and* ANGUS *holds up a warning finger. They wait motionless except for* RHONA's *jaw, still chewing*)

(*An* ANNOUNCER's *voice is heard speaking through a mike back stage*)

ANNOUNCER. Good afternoon, ladies and gentlemen. Once again we present "The Starchers—the story of just an ordinary farmer's family"!

(ANGUS *still keeps his finger poised and then. as the red light comes on steady, brings it down.* GWLADYS *nods regally and begins to read from her script. She has to hold it arms-length and read it through her lorgnettes*)

GWLADYS (*but now in the broadest country accent she can muster*) Ah, well, Dan'l, I've always said we're just a great big 'appy family 'ere at Meadowsweet Farm.
ANGUS (*holding his script as close to his face as he can and using his monocle like a magnifying glass*) Ar! (*He hastily produces a throat spray and uses it on himself*)
GWLADYS. But I'm warnin' you, Dan'l Starcher, there'll be trouble if I don't get a new overall in place of this ragged filthy ole thing! (*She twitches her sables contemptuously*) I'm ashamed to wear it.
ANGUS (*having lost his place in the script, finds it again*) Ar!
GWLADYS. Dan'l—you ain't payin' no 'eed to me. What're you doin'?
ANGUS (*also broad Mummerset*) Tryin' to piece out there 'ere forms from the Government. As you know, Doris, I never 'ad no

book-larnin' like, an' I'm proper foxed by readin' matter. Look —what's this word—C.O.W.—what does that spell to you?

(GWLADYS *looks hard at* RHONA *who scowls back*)

GWLADYS. Grace!
ANGUS. Eh?
GWLADYS. It's Grace, Dan'l. Young Grace Freebody, come to see us.
RHONA (*in the most timidly genteel accents*) Hullo, Mr Starcher, how are you?
ANGUS. Ooo, same as usual, thank'ee, Grace. Fit as a fiddle! (*He takes a hasty pill*) Never 'ad a day's illness in me life. (*He takes a stethoscope out and listens anxiously to his chest*)
RHONA. That's a very nice dress you're wearing, Mrs Starcher.
GWLADYS (*exposing her fabulous dress*) What—this ole rag? Why, I run this up out of a flour sack twenty-five years ago.
RHONA. Well, if you like, *I* could make a dress for you. My friends say I have very good taste in clothes.

(GWLADYS *raises very disdainful eyebrows at* RHONA's *outfit*)

ANGUS. Ar, well, that'd depend 'ow much you charge, Grace.

(*In a flash,* RHONA *opens her bag and distributes cards to the men*)

RHONA (*coyly*) 'Course there'd be no charge to *you*, Mr Starcher.
ANGUS. Ar, well, we'll talk about that later. I jest want to 'ave a word with ole Walter Gamaliel first—hoy, Walter!
HILARY (*in deep hoarse Mummerset*) Oo-ar-ee-oo—how do, Mester Starcher! (*He draws languidly on his jade holder*)
GWLADYS. Walter—I wish you wouldn't smoke in here. I can't stand that 'orrible shag o' yourn.
HILARY. Well, you know what they say, Mrs Starcher. Strong baccy for strong men.
ANGUS (*laughing merrily*) That's you all right, Walter. Proper ole son o' the sod you are and no mistake. 'Ere—by the way. 'Ow's your King Edwards?
HILARY. Oo-ar-ee-oo, they're a rare ole size this year, Mr Starcher. It ain't them I'm frettin' about. It's Daisy.
ANGUS. Daisy? Why? What's wrong with the old gal?
HILARY. Well, look at 'er—she's just comin'—look . . . 'Ullo, Daisy!

(*Everyone moves away from the mike as* DYMPHNA *steps up and solemnly intones into it*)

DYMPHNA. Mmmmmoooo-ooo!

(*After which, she folds her script neatly, leaves the mike, goes over and collects all her belongings and walks sedately off the stage*)

GWLADYS. Ar—I don't like the look of her fetlocks.

RHONA. I doubt if *she'll* yield any more.
ANGUS. Never mind 'er, Walter—'ave you done that muck-spreading over by the pigsty yet?
HILARY (*shuddering in horror*) Oo-ar-ee-oo. No, I ain't, Mr Starcher.
GWLADYS. You can do it when you take the swill over, Walter. There's a nice ole bucket of mouldy bread and cold gravy I mixed for you in the scullery.
HILARY (*looking very ill and passing a shaking hand over his forehead*) Oo-ar.
ANGUS. An' when you done that you can worm ole Rover. An' if you got time, clean out that slaughter'ouse. It's a proper mess with all them ole tripes 'anging around.
HILARY (*who has been getting steadily sicker throughout this—very faintly*) Oo-ar-ee-oo!

(HILARY *pulls out a bright silk handkerchief, claps it over his mouth, and with a final heartfelt* "Ooh" *he exits hurriedly*)
ANGUS (*comfortably*) Ar, it's a good job we got ole Walter for the rough stuff. 'E's good enough for *ten* men, 'e is. Why . . .
GWLADYS. 'Ere—'oo's that coming over the ten acre field? (*She holds her script even further away to get it in focus*) You 'ave a look, Dan'l—you got better eyes 'n what I have.
ANGUS (*with his script even closer to his face*) Well, 'e's about five mile away, but it looks to me like young Phil—yes, it is. 'E's ad an 'aircut I see.
GWLADYS. Ar, so that's why you're 'ere, Grace. Waitin' for your young man.
ANGUS. Ar! 'E's coming this way too. (*He suddenly realizes that Mr Croot is still asleep. He yells*) *I said* 'e's coming this way!

(RHONA *and* GWLADYS *dash over and rouse* MR CROOT *who comes to, and totters mumbling towards the mike, supported by the ladies*)

(*Frantically ad libbing and swallowing nerve tonic*) Oo, ar, 'e's comin' this way all right. 'E ain't 'arf in an 'urry too. 'E's runnin' all the way. Coo—did you see 'im jump that 'edge down by the sheep dip? Ar, 'ere 'e is. Come on in, Phil!

(*But* MR CROOT *is too exhausted by his journey to do more than croak feebly at the mike*)

Ar, I reckon you're a bit puffed after your run, aincher?

(MR CROOT *who is being fanned by* RHONA *nods feebly*)

Well, runnin' won't do you no 'arm—a well set-up young feller like you—especially when there's a pretty gal at the end of it, eh, Phil?

(*He pokes* MR CROOT *jocularly in the ribs. This is a mistake, since*

MR CROOT *immediately collapses. The ladies try to bring him round without success*)

ANGUS. Well, come along, Phil—aincher you got anything to say for yourself?

(*The two ladies shake their heads sadly at* ANGUS *who looks frantically at the mike and then beckons feverishly to the wings. And from the wings comes the most countryfied yokel you ever saw. Smock, gaiters, leggings, shock of hair hanging down from a ragged old slouch hat, straw in the mouth, idiot grin revealing several blacked-out teeth, and large, round apple-red cheeks. He walks up to the mike and speaks*)

YOKEL (*in the most cultured Oxford accent possible*) Ladies and gentlemen, you have just heard the one millionth episode of "The Starchers"!

BLACK-OUT

PETER PATTER

Words by　　　　　　　　　　*Music by*
DAVID CLIMIE　　　　　　　JOHN PRITCHETT

Characters

A YOUNG MAN　　*Hugh Paddick*
A YOUNG LADY　　*Joan Heal*

The scene is a restaurant. Down stage there are a table and two chairs. A YOUNG MAN *is discovered standing near the table; he is anxiously consulting his watch. A* YOUNG LADY *enters, takes one look at the man, rushes over and starts talking to him at top speed. Throughout the number the man opens his mouth to reply to every question, but he hardly ever succeeds in getting a word in edgeways.*

LADY. Peter Parsons, as I live and breathe!
　　　　　　　　　　　　　Well, fancy meeting you!
　　You remember me, of course—I'm Sally Hughes!
　　It must be ten years since we met—but you haven't changed, my pet.
　　Come on—sit down and tell me *all* your news . . .
　　(*She drags him to the table and sits down with him*)
MAN. Well . . .
LADY. Oh, Peter, Peter, *Peter*, you just *couldn't* be looking sweeter!
　　Are you keeping fit? Well, obviously you are.
　　How long are you in town? Don't you think *I'm* looking brown?
　　I've been down to Monte Carlo in the car.
　　Have you ever been to Monte? Isn't it sweet?
　　　　　　　　　　　　　I went with Auntie—
　　You remember Auntie May—wasn't she a yell?
　　She's the one you used to say looked just like your dappled grey—
　　Whatever *happened* to that horse, dear?
MAN.　　　　　　　　　　　　　　　　Well . . .
LADY. Remember our last ride, dear—when you had that lovely idea
　　And I got home with my jodhpurs soaked in dew?
　　Wasn't Daddy furious? And yet, you know, it's curious
　　I've never felt ashamed of it—have you?

INTIMACY AT EIGHT-THIRTY

Well, really, there's no need to—I've just never paid much heed to
The conventions—or the penalties incurred—
So you *mustn't* say you're sorry for that evening in the quarry,
No, please, my dear—don't *say* another word!
Oh, Peter, Peter, Peter, isn't it marvellous to meet a
Childhood sweetheart—don't you think? Of course you do.
Remember when we parted? Weren't you simply broken-hearted?
Well, naturally you were, my dear—me too!
Remember telling mother we were made for one another?
She didn't believe us, did she? But it's true.
And you're still my fav'rite flame—I don't suppose you feel the same,
Or do you?

MAN. Well . . .
LADY. Peter, dear, you *do*!
So *that's* the torch you carried? Do you mean you never married?
You didn't? Peter darling, nor did I.
I just saved myself for you, dear—no, I felt I wanted to, dear . . .

(*The* MAN *buries his head in his hands desperately*)

Oh, Peter, darling Peter—please don't cry.
No more need for tears and sorrow—sweet, I'll marry you tomorrow.
Is that all right? No—say the twenty-third.
(*Tearfully*) No, Peter, dear, don't thank me—just let me find my hankie—
No, please, my dear—don't *say* another word.

MAN (*desperately*) Well . . .
LADY. Oh, Peter, Peter, *Peter*, my life *couldn't* be completer!
Let's start making plans, dear, right away.
Do you want a quiet wedding? I must see about some bedding—
Or could we stay a while with Auntie May?
No—straight after the marriage we can catch the train to Harwich,
And we'll stay with Mummy for a month or two.

MAN. Well . . .
LADY. You needn't look like *that*—Mummy's got a *lovely* flat,
And I'm sure she's always most polite to *you*.
Very diff'rent from your *mother*—and your nasty little brother—

You've got *very* little room to sneer and scoff.
I won't sit here like a dummy while you insult poor Mummy—
If you feel like that we'd better call it off!
Oh, I'm glad you spoke your mind out, and I'm very glad to find out
What you're like before the wedding day occurred—
And to think you nearly lured me into marriage—well, that's cured me—
Oh, no, my dear—don't *say* another word!

(*The* MAN *in desperation produces a card and thrusts it on her*)

I suggest we say "Good-bye"—what's this? Your card? But why?
(*She reads it*) Mr Henry Arthur Brown! But that's absurd!

(*She reads it*)

You mean that you're *not* Peter?

(*The* MAN *shakes his head*)

Well, you might have been discreeter!
That's the most ill-mannered thing I ever heard!
How could *you* sit there and just *never* say a word?

(*She exits in high dudgeon*)

BLACK-OUT

www.ingramcontent.com/pod-product-compliance
Ingram Content Group UK Ltd.
Pitfield, Milton Keynes, MK11 3LW, UK
UKHW021840210426